Leni Sonnenfeld

Beside the Jordan.

*Leni Sonnenfeld*

THE

# JORDAN

*River of the Promised Land*

## by VIOLET WEINGARTEN

*Map by Fred Kliem*

**GARRARD PUBLISHING COMPANY**
*CHAMPAIGN, ILLINOIS*

NANCY LARRICK, ED.D.,
IS THE EDUCATIONAL ADVISOR FOR THIS SERIES

*Herbert S. Sonnenfeld*

Boating on the Jordan near Kibbutz Degania.

# Contents

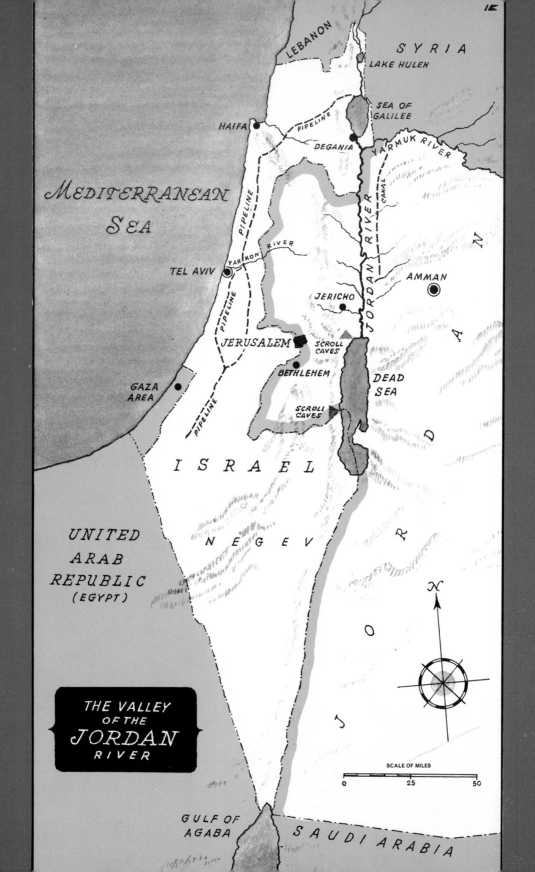

LEBANON

SYRIA

LAKE HULEH

*MEDITERRANEAN
SEA*

HAIFA

PIPELINE

SEA OF
GALILEE

DEGANIA

YARMUK RIVER

CANAL

JORDAN RIVER

PIPELINE

PIPELINE

YARKON RIVER

TEL AVIV

AMMAN

JERICHO

PIPELINE

JERUSALEM

SCROLL
CAVES

BETHLEHEM

DEAD
SEA

GAZA
AREA

PIPELINE

I S R A E L

SCROLL
CAVES

J   O   R   D   A   N

UNITED
ARAB
REPUBLIC
(EGYPT)

N E G E V

N

J

THE VALLEY
OF THE
JORDAN
RIVER

SCALE OF MILES

0          25          50

GULF OF
AGABA

SAUDI ARABIA

# 1. A David Among Goliaths

A poor shepherd boy named David once lived near the River Jordan. He was small and scrawny, but he killed a giant named Goliath with a single stone and became a king.

The Jordan is like a David among rivers. Next to giants like the Nile and the Mississippi, it is puny. Its course is less than 200 miles, and in some places it is as narrow as 25 feet. Travelers are always surprised to see how small a river it is.

But the Jordan flows through one of the most fascinating valleys in the world. Its brief course takes it from snow to desert. It winds through the deepest gorge on earth and ends in the lowest lake. Every day the Jordan pours over 6,000,000 tons of water into a sea with no outlet, that never overflows because the water evaporates as fast as it comes in. The Jordan is a freshwater stream, but at its mouth its waters are five times saltier than the ocean.

Nowhere else is there such a wide variety of animal life and vegetation in so small a space. Mountain bears, wild boars, jackals, and gazelles are found near the river. There are thousands of species of plants—subarctic ferns, hollyhocks like those in English gardens, and tropical palm trees.

Men have lived beside the Jordan since prehistoric times. A few years ago a Galilee farmer working with a bulldozer turned up the bones of a man who had lived in the valley from 500,000 to 600,000 years ago. Flint axes dating back to 100,000 B.C. can be picked up on the shore. The tusk of an elephant who trampled its rushes 50,000 years ago was found in the mud of the riverbed.

The valley has the ruins of a 4,000-year-old underground city complete with galleries, granaries, furnished caves, and wells. All were built 30 feet below ground as a refuge from the summer heat

The river turns and twists through a fascinating valley.

and winter damp. Nearby are a twentieth-century nuclear power plant and a research center where scientists work to make artificial rain. Nowhere else can you cover so much history in so small a space.

The narrow strip through which the Jordan

7

Archeologists uncover a series of columns near Hazor in Israel.

flows is a bridge between Asia and Africa. The oldest road in the world, the caravan route from Egypt to Damascus, fords the river in the north. The area used to be known as Palestine. Countless armies have battled over it. The Jordan has seen Babylonians, Assyrians, Egyptians, Ethiopians, Hittites, Parthians, Persians, Greeks, Romans, Mongols, Turks, the French, and the British.

It is still a battlefield. In 1948 the United Nations proposed that Palestine be divided into a Jewish and an Arab state. The Jewish state is

Israel. The Arab state is part of the Kingdom of Jordan. The Israelis, descendants of the ancient Hebrew settlers of Palestine, and the Arabs of the surrounding country are fighting over the use of water from the Jordan River.

The Jordan is an archaeologist's dream. In fact, archaeology is almost a national sport in Israel. Families go digging the way Americans go to baseball games. Israel is smaller than Vermont, but it has over 60 archaeological museums and collections. Jordan, on the east side of the river, has been called an "open-air museum."

Many of the events described in the Bible took place near the River Jordan. Jesus preached beside

This ancient carved stone is decorated with Judaic symbols.

*Leni Sonnenfeld*

the Sea of Galilee, through which the Jordan flows, and He was baptized in the river. To this day, babies in churches throughout the world are baptized with water brought from the Jordan in memory of Jesus.

Men have always loved the Jordan. Shepherds guarding their flocks in Old Testament times sang songs in its praise. Its waters were said to have healing powers. Oppressed people read Bible stories about how the ancient children of Israel crossed the Jordan to freedom and found hope. Many of the songs we sing are about the Jordan. "Swing Low, Sweet Chariot" has a verse that begins, "I looked over Jordan . . ." One song says, "Roll, Jordan, Roll!" And still another refers to the Jordan as "Deep River." It is a good description, even though the Jordan is not really a deep river. When it comes to importance, the Jordan's waters run deep.

Palm trees line the shore of Lake Huleh today.

## 2. The Lion in the Snow

The Bible has a puzzle about a youth named Benaiah who killed a lion in the snow. How could a jungle beast be found in snow? It would be hard to solve that puzzle anywhere except in the Jordan Valley. Before lions became extinct there, it was possible for a lion to look for a cool spot on a hot day, get lost, and end up in snowy mountains. No other river changes altitude and, therefore, climates, as quickly as the Jordan. Its name in Hebrew—*Yarden*—means "the river that goes down." The Arabs call it *Al Urdunn*, "The Descender."

The Jordan rises in mountains 9,000 feet above sea level. Less than 160 miles farther south, it comes to a bitter end in the salty Dead Sea. This is the lowest spot on earth: 1,286 feet below sea level. In its brief journey, the river passes hills, valleys, gorges, fields, jungles, swamps, orchards, and a hallowed lake. It twists in rapids and whirlpools, and meanders gently. Its waters can be crystal clear, muddy, deep-green, pale-blue, or the fleeting rainbow color of an oil slick on a wet road.

The bed of the Jordan lies in the biggest crack in the earth's crust. This crack—the Great Rift—extends from northern Syria across the Red Sea into Africa. The headwaters of the river flow down from Mount Hermon in southern Syria. Mount Hermon is always topped with snow. In ancient times the snow was collected to cool the drinks of the rich.

According to a Hebrew legend, Mount Hermon was once only a little hill. But when God gave the Ten Commandments to Moses on Mount Sinai, Mount Hermon was so upset at being overlooked that it wept. God made the mountain tall to console it, and the tears it shed became the Jordan.

12

*Leni Sonnenfeld*

**Along parts of the river, bamboo and papyrus thrive in the jungle.**

Three small streams—the Hasbani in Lebanon, the Banias in Syria and the Dan in Israel—feed the Jordan at its source. The Banias springs out of a mysterious-looking cave. The ancient Greeks, who were among the many conquerors of the area, believed the cave was sacred to their woodland god Pan and his nymphs. To this day you can see the inscription they carved in Greek over the entrance to the cave: PANI TE KAI NYMPHIAS, "To Pan and the Nymphs." They called the sparkling little stream Panias after Pan. There is no P in

13

*Leni Sonnenfeld*

Lava blocked the river to form Lake Huleh and vast swamps.

the Arab alphabet, so when the Arabs took over, Panias became Banias.

Aeons ago, volcanic eruptions poured tons of lava into the Jordan Valley just after the river leaves Mount Hermon. The lava blocked the river so that it flooded its banks and formed swamps and a small lake called Huleh. Great papyrus jungles, some sixteen feet high, flourished in the swamps. Water buffalo and wild boars rooted among the yellow water lilies. Caravans of birds swarmed overhead. But beautiful as Lake Huleh was, it was also a breeding place for malaria-bearing mosquitoes. Millions of gallons of precious water were wasted there.

In 1957 the Israeli government completed a

Swamps were drained (above) to make rich farmland shown below.

*Israel Information Services*

seven-year project to drain the swamps and the lake. They dug out the ancient lava and freed the course of the river. Now the Jordan rides through 15,000 acres of rice fields, sugar-cane plantations, flower gardens, and silver-blue fishponds stocked with carp. There are 40 neat villages in the new Huleh Valley. But the migrating birds still come, for a portion of the old Huleh was kept as a game preserve. Some of the papyrus swamp was saved, too, because this is one of the few places where papyrus still grows.

After Huleh, the Jordan drops 900 feet in nine miles. The landscape is desolate. To the east lie the bleak, yellow-gray Syrian hills. To the west are barren reddish rock outcroppings. Before the Israelis can do any planting, they have to move great boulders, some weighing as much as a ton.

Then the Jordan waters mingle with the sapphire-blue Sea of Galilee. This small fresh-water sea used to be called Lake Kinneret because it is shaped like a *kinnor*, or harp. That is still its name in Hebrew. The lake, lying 700 feet below sea level, has always been known for its beauty

The Jordan pours into Lake Kinneret, also called the Sea of Galilee.

and its gentle climate. The Hebrews had a saying that "God created seven seas but the Sea of Galilee was his delight." In early spring after the rains, the hills around the lake are covered with almond blossoms, oleanders, red and purple anemones, cyclamen, scarlet poppies, and wild tulips. In March cranes fly over it, heading for Russia after spending the winter in central Africa. Kingfishers, herons, and pelicans dip into the fish-laden waters.

The Jordan pours out of the Sea of Galilee like

water from a funnel. South of the lake, it is joined by its main tributary, the Yarmuk River, which forms the boundary between Israel and Jordan for about eight miles. For the rest of its 73-mile journey through Israel, the Jordan zigzags through reclaimed farmland. One of these farms is called "Sam's Farm," after a California farmer named Sam Hamburger, who grew the first cotton in Israel here. Except during the spring floods, the Jordan is never more than five feet deep after it leaves the Sea of Galilee.

The river drops another 600 feet as it twists through the valley. The distance from the Sea of Galilee to the Dead Sea is less than 65 miles as the crow flies. But the river writhes like a snake, so it actually travels 200 miles to the Dead Sea after leaving the Sea of Galilee.

In Biblical times, this serpentine section was called the "Jungle of the Jordan." It is a harsh place. Winters are warm and brief, with little rain. Summer is burning hot and dry. Spring and fall bring *Khamsin* days. *Khamsin* means "fifty" in Arabic. The dry, dust-laden, blinding desert wind

Herbert S. Sonnenfeld

This is believed to be the spot where Jesus was baptized.

that raises temperatures to over 120 degrees Fahrenheit is given that name because it is said to blow for fifty days once it starts.

Past the jungle thickets, the river becomes gentle again. Here, a few miles below King Husayn Bridge, between two green stretches of shore, lined with tamarisks and willows, is the spot where it is said Jesus was baptized. Pilgrims have

These Americans are being baptized in the Sea of Galilee.

Wide World

come here to bathe since the fourth century. During a single day in the Middle Ages, 60,000 people were said to have plunged into the river. Looking at it today, it is hard to see where there was room for them all. When the Czars ruled Russia, Russian pilgrims used to come to dip themselves in the river, wearing white gowns that they saved to be used as their burial robes.

During the rainy season, of course, the Jordan looks muddy and brown, even at the place of baptism. That explains the Biblical story of Naaman's scorn for the Jordan. Naaman, an important Syrian general, suffered a disfiguring skin disease. A wise Hebrew called Elisha told Naaman to wash himself in the Jordan seven times if he wished to be cured.

The Syrian general was furious. "Are not Abanah and Pharpar, the rivers of Damascus, better than all the waters of Israel?" he raged. He acted exactly the way a man from Colorado would if he were told to leave his clear mountain streams and wash himself in the muddy Mississippi.

But Naaman swallowed his pride and dipped

himself into the Jordan seven times. The seventh time he came up, his skin was whole and sound again.

Naaman was lucky that he was not told to dip himself in the Jordan a little farther south. That is where the Jordan comes to an end in the brackish Dead Sea. It pours 6,000,000 tons of water into the sea every day. In the winter, torrents flow in from the hills as well. From this point on, the only outlet for the water of the Jordan is evaporation. Most of the nearby land is dead and useless.

There is one green exception, however. It is Musa Alami's farm school for Arab boys made homeless when Palestine was divided. Convinced that there had to be fresh water somewhere under the surface of the parched land, Musa Alami spent six months digging wells and in January of 1950 struck water. He used the water for irrigation and as soon as he got his first crop in, he founded his school. Now Musa Alami's farm and 160 homeless boys flourish. There is even a big swimming pool near the flowering orchard.

No birds fly over the Dead Sea because it has no fish or plants.

# 3. Americans Explore a Mystery

The 48-mile-long Dead Sea has been called the most horrible spot on earth. Its surface lies farther below sea level than a coal mine. At its greatest depth, it is nearly 2,600 feet below sea level. It is the lowest natural spot known. Barren limestone cliffs, that look like twisted metal in the glare of the broiling sun, surround it. Rock salt, lava, and sulfur streak its shores, and patches of slime float on its oily waters. In medieval times its vapors were thought to be poisonous, and the

Arabs long believed that birds died in the attempt to fly across it.

All in all, if you wanted to pick a place where something terrible could happen, you would pick the Dead Sea. Perhaps you would be right. One of the greatest calamities of all time happened here, according to the Old Testament, and traces of that calamity are visible yet.

According to the Bible, the shore of the Dead Sea used to be a fertile plain. It had five lovely towns. Among them were Sodom and Gomorrah. The people of Sodom and Gomorrah were so wicked that God decided to destroy them. But there was one good man whose name was Lot. God did not want to punish him so he sent two angels to warn him to flee with his family. Once Lot did so, the Bible says, "The Lord rained upon Sodom and upon Gomorrah brimstone and fire. And He overthrew those cities, and all the plain, and all the inhabitants of those cities, and that which grew upon the ground."

Ever since then, men have pointed to Sodom and Gomorrah as examples of how great cities could be laid waste because of their wickedness. But until about a century ago, no one really knew whether the story of Sodom and Gomorrah was anything more than just that—a very good story.

In 1848 the United States sent a group of scientists headed by Lieutenant Commander W. F. Lynch to study the strange, landlocked sea. The expedition intended to investigate the story of the rain of "brimstone and fire." They wanted to test the poisonous gases.

In addition, the scientists knew of two other strange stories about the Dead Sea. One was about the wife of the good man Lot. The Old Testament reports that the angels had warned Lot and his family not to look back when they left Sodom, but Lot's wife became curious. She turned around and ". . . she became a pillar of salt."

The other story dated from the time of the Roman occupation of the Jordan Valley. Titus, a Roman general, had thrown three slaves bound together with chains into the Dead Sea, but they did not sink. Instead they bobbed to the surface; whereupon Titus gave them their freedom.

The American scientists came equipped with two metal boats, which they launched on the Sea of Galilee, and worked their way downriver from there. It was a long hot trip because of the river's zigzag course. When the scientists finally arrived at the point where the Jordan empties into the Dead Sea, they felt they had earned a swim. They jumped into the water—and nearly popped out. Obviously the story about Titus and the slaves was true. What was the explanation?

The Americans spent 22 days on the Dead Sea. They tested the water, took soundings, searched for fish, and then drew up a report.

For the first time it was revealed that the Dead

It is almost impossible not to float on the Dead Sea.
*Vagn Hansen—Black Star*

Brushwood is carried by camel and donkey in the Dead Sea area.

Sea has no outlet. The heat there is so intense that over 280,000,000 cubic feet of water evaporate each day. The water that is left contains about 25 percent solid matter—mostly salt—as compared with 5 percent in the Atlantic and other oceans. The solid matter makes people float. (Modern tourists often have their pictures taken lying on the water reading a paper.)

It is true there are no fish in the Dead Sea. It is too salty. Any fish that do slip in from the Jordan are killed in a minute. Birds do not fly over the lake because it contains no fish or plant life for them to eat.

There is a range of hills made of pure rock salt at the southern shore of the Dead Sea. Arabs mine salt there to this day, and the Arabic name for the range, *Jebel Usdum*, has the sound of "Sodom" in it if you say it aloud. Blocks of salt, loosened by rain, stand on end, some looking sculptured. One of these blocks is actually called "Lot's Wife."

One hundred years after those first American scientists came to the Dead Sea, another group of scientists investigated the same area. They were from the Smithsonian Institution in Washington, D.C., and the American School of Oriental Research in Jerusalem. They used the very latest scientific instruments and knowledge. They concluded that at one time the surface of the Dead Sea had been 1,400 feet above its present level, higher than the Mediterranean Sea. It had covered an expanse of about 200 miles with fresh water. But when the earth's crust split into that deep, bold gash which is the Great Rift, the Dead Sea dropped. It came into contact with salt deposits deep in the earth, thus becoming so salty

that all living matter within it died immediately.

In addition, the Jordan brings to the lake all the minerals it collects on its journey. When the water evaporates, the salts are left behind. Now the lake is estimated to contain one thousand million tons of magnesium, bromide, and potash as well as common salt. It is one of the world's biggest sources of potash.

The scientists also found an explanation for the story of Sodom and Gomorrah. They located evidence of volcanic activity around the Dead Sea, as in the rest of the Jordan Valley. Geological studies showed that there had been a great earthquake in the area about 1900 B.C. The earthquake hit the base of the Great Rift fracture on the southern shore, just about where Sodom and Gomorrah were supposed to be. Then the waters rose and covered whatever had been there.

Beside the Dead Sea today there are scattered youth hostels, mineral-extracting plants, an air-conditioned resort hotel, and even a post office—the lowest post office in the world. But they

Rocks are eroded by wind and sand
into weird formations.
*Trans World Airlines Photo*

appear swallowed up in the general desolation. The southern shore looks as barren as ever. And if the sun happens to be in the right place, it is possible to see outlines of ancient trees under the surface of the shallow waters. For years they have been preserved in the strong salts. Perhaps Lot's children played under those trees, or his angel visitors rested there.

Trans World Airlines Photo
An Israeli looks across the Dead Sea to the hills of Jordan.

The Ark carried around the walls of Jericho.

## 4. Joshua Fights a Battle

As the smoke rose from Sodom and Gomorrah, Lot's uncle, Abraham, was watching from a nearby hill. According to the Old Testament, it was because of Abraham that God sent the angels to warn Lot away from Sodom. Abraham had a very special relationship with God. He was the first person in history to believe in one Almighty God.

Probably Abraham arrived at this belief while

31

he tended sheep under the broad, star-filled skies of his native Mesopotamia. The people around him worshiped many gods. But Abraham could not. So he left Mesopotamia with his family and flocks and came to the land then called Canaan, west of the Jordan River. The Canaanites called Abraham *Ibri*, meaning "he who came from across the river." His family, including his nephew Lot, came to be known as *Ibrim*, or Hebrews. Modern Israel, which includes Canaan, traces its name back to Abraham's grandson, Israel. Hebrews, in turn, are now called Jews, after Judah, Israel's son.

In Canaan, Abraham and his people continued to live as shepherds. But their belief in one God made them different from the other people around them. The three great religions based on belief in one God—the Jewish, Christian, and Islamic— all owe that belief to the extraordinary shepherd, Abraham, who lived beside the Jordan. The Hebrews prospered in Canaan.

Then, years after Abraham died, there was a great famine. Possibly the Jordan ran low. The wells ran dry. Many of the Hebrews moved to

Wide World

Even today women get water from Elisha's fountain in Jericho.

Egypt, where they had heard there was plenty of pasture. They remained in Egypt for hundreds of years. Toward the end of that period, they remained unwillingly, for they had become slaves. Finally a great leader, Moses, promised to lead them back to the Jordan Valley. Here was land which God, in the time of Abraham, had given them for "an everlasting possession."

With the help of God, Moses led the Hebrews in their escape from Egypt. Once, with pursuing Egyptians at their backs, the Hebrews found themselves trapped on the shores of the Sea of Reeds with no boats. At God's order, the Bible says, Moses told the waters to part and the Hebrews walked to the other side. When the Egyptians tried to walk after them, the waters closed and drowned them.

It took 40 years for the Hebrews to get back to their Promised Land. They wandered through deserts and were so hungry at times that God sent them a food called manna. They climbed jagged mountains. Sometimes their search for water took them miles out of their way. At other times they had to detour to avoid enemy tribes. The result was that although they had started out from Egypt far west of the Jordan River, they ended up approaching Canaan from the east bank of the river.

By this time, according to the Old Testament, Moses was 120 years old. He knew that the time had come for him to die. But he also knew that God had promised him that he would see Canaan first, even if it was not meant for him to go there. So he climbed to the top of Mount Nebo, and from there he saw the "land of milk and honey" to which he had led his people. He gazed at "the plain of the valley of Jericho, the city of palm trees, and then," says the Bible, "Moses, the servant of the Lord, died."

The Hebrews remained on the east bank of the river for a month, mourning. Then God spoke to Joshua, the sturdy young man Moses had picked to succeed him, and said, "Now therefore arise, go over this Jordan, thou and all this people, unto the land which I do give them."

This was a tall order. Canaan was inhabited by a strong, powerful people. It had well-fortified cities, especially the great walled city of Jericho. The Jordan, then in flood, acted as a water-filled moat. The Hebrews were weak after their wandering. They had few weapons and not a single boat. But Joshua, like Moses, trusted in his God.

He told the Hebrews to get ready. He had twelve stones placed in the middle of the river. Then he instructed the Jewish priests to take the Ark of the Covenant, the boxlike structure in which the Spirit of God was said to live, and stand on the stones. As soon as the feet of the priests touched the stones, the waters of the Jordan rolled toward the north and the waters of the Salt Sea, or the Dead Sea, rolled to the south. Then 40,000 Hebrews, standing back 3,000 feet from the Ark, marched over the riverbed without wetting so much as a sandal.

Meanwhile, Joshua had sent spies into Jericho. They came back with news that the people of Jericho had closed the city gates and manned its walls. The Canaanites were already uneasy about the Hebrews because they had heard the story of how God had parted the sea for them on the coast of Egypt, a generation earlier. Now that they had seen the miracle of the River Jordan, they were terrified. Joshua was delighted with the news. He decided to use the Canaanites' fear as a weapon against them, waging what we call psychological warfare today.

First, Joshua lined up his desert-hardened fighters outside the thick red walls of Jericho. In front of them he put seven priests carrying trumpets made of rams' horns, the same trumpets that are blown to this day on certain Jewish holy

The fall of the walls of Jericho (from an old engraving).

days. Priests and soldiers marched once around the city, silently. Then, to the astonishment of the watching people of Jericho, they returned to their camp. Next day they did the same thing. And the next day. And the next. In all, they circled the walls of Jericho silently six days in a row.

By this time, the people of Jericho did not know what to think. Had the Hebrews gone mad, or

Archaeologists have uncovered walls of Jericho dating to 6,000 B.C.

did they know something the Canaanites did not?

On the seventh day, Joshua rose at dawn and dressed carefully. He led his warriors and the seven priests to the walls of Jericho. The Hebrew people, aware that something special was going to happen, crowded in behind them. This time the soldiers marched around the walls seven times, and the priests blew mightily on the trumpets. The seventh time around, the priests gave a long blast, following orders Joshua had given them. At the sound of the blast, Joshua called out to the Hebrews: "Shout; for the Lord hath given you the city!" Then the people gave a great shout, and the walls crumbled completely. The Hebrews marched in, and the city and the Promised Land that went with it was theirs.

In the words of the rousing spiritual:

> Joshua fit the battle of Jericho, Jericho,
> Joshua fit the battle of Jericho,
> And the walls came tumbling down!

The story of Joshua is one of the great stories in the Bible. But just as in the case of Sodom and Gomorrah, hundreds of years later many people doubted that it had ever happened. After all, there is another story that Joshua once ordered the sun to stand still so that he could finish a battle in daylight—and it did. Sensible people do not believe in the sun's standing still, rivers parting and walls falling down on order. Besides, there were no remains of the city of Jericho where it was supposed to have existed.

The only Jericho people could see consisted of ruins of a town built by the Romans when they ruled the area. This town had a story, too. When the Roman general Mark Antony captured it, he gave its gardens to the Egyptian queen Cleopatra. These gardens were famous for their balsam trees that yielded a spicy-smelling substance called balm. In ancient times balm was swallowed as a medicine and applied to wounds. Cleopatra had some of the balsam trees brought to her own gardens in Egypt. Then she rented the gardens to the local Roman governor, Herod, for about $150,000 in our money. After a while Herod got tired of paying rent, so he confiscated the gardens. Then he built himself a Roman town beside the balsam trees.

After the Romans left, Jericho became a sleepy little desert town.

Then in 1873, American and British archaeologists came to dig in the Jordan Valley. They got to work on a nearby mound of ruins called Tell-es-Sultan, and before long their spades turned over some obviously old bricks. They dug deeper and made an amazing discovery. Another Jericho not only had existed, but there had been many

*Trans World Airlines Photo*
Above ground you can see these remains of the walls of Jericho.

Jerichos, for there were signs of still earlier cities under the ancient site.

Since then, archaeologists have continued to excavate at old Jericho. The site looks like half of a giant club sandwich, with each layer going back further into time. It now appears that Jericho was an old city by the time Moses saw it and Joshua lined up his men outside its walls. It was even an old city when their ancestor Abraham came to Canaan.

Jericho goes back at least to 7,000 B.C. It is the oldest known city site. The pyramids of Egypt,

41

The modern city of Jericho lies in Jordan north of the Dead Sea.

the first great structures of the Nile Valley, are 4,000 years younger than the round tower and steps at Jericho. The early inhabitants of Jericho seem to have had a system for irrigating fields in which they grew some of man's earliest grain. Kathleen Kenyon, the British archaeologist in charge of the "dig," says they made bricks by hand. They were shaped like a flat cigar, with a pattern formed by the brickmakers' thumbs. On the basis of the findings at Jericho, it is now generally agreed that the Jordan Valley is one of the birthplaces of civilization. Here men stopped being savages, hunting game and gathering wild grain, and began a settled life.

Other towns were built on top of that first Jericho town. The site, an oasis, was too precious to abandon. The town that was the Jericho of Joshua's time—about the thirteenth century B.C.—turned out to have double walls. The outer wall was five feet thick, the inner one ten feet thick. Between the two walls was a narrow gangway on which soldiers could stand. The walls show great cracks. Sections of both walls look as if a giant hand rose between them and pushed them apart until they fell.

So it does seem that the walls of Jericho did fall in the time of Joshua. The only question is how. Archaeologists have evidence that five other cities were destroyed during the same period on the west bank of the Jordan. Was there a great earthquake? Did an earth tremor shatter the walls of Jericho by coincidence just at the moment the trumpets blared and the people shouted? Did the vibration of the marching feet tumble the shaking walls? Or was there a miracle?

While you think about it, you might be interested to know that we have proof of earthquake activity in the area in comparatively recent times. Only three miles from ancient Jericho lie the ruins of an immense palace built A.D. 724 by a powerful Arab prince. Desert-born, he hated the dampness of his capital city, Damascus, so he moved his court to the Jordan Valley every winter. He built his palace with great pools, steam baths, gardens, and courtyards. He decorated it with beautiful statues and mosaics. An earthquake shook it to pieces.

One more thing to think about: Was it a miracle that made the waters of the Jordan dry up to let the Hebrews cross over? Or is there an explanation for that, too? It is a fact that in 1927 a cliff fell into the Jordan near Jericho and dammed its water for an entire day.

# 5. The Caves of the Jordan

Even if there were nothing above ground in the Jordan Valley, it would still be interesting because of its caves.

The history of the ancient Kingdom of Israel begins and ends in three of these caves.

The first cave is near an oasis called Ein Gedi, which means "the Stream of the Kid," on the western shore of the Dead Sea. That is where David, the shepherd boy, proved himself worthy of being king.

The Hebrews had just chosen a tribesman named Saul as their first king. Saul made young David a captain in his first army because of the brave way he killed the giant Goliath with his slingshot.

Then Saul became jealous of David. He exiled him. With a loyal band of followers, David hid out in the caves near Ein Gedi, like a Jewish Robin Hood. His deeds angered the king even more so he decided to put an end to David. Accompanied by an army, Saul came to Ein Gedi to seize him. After hours of searching the limestone cliffs, Saul decided to rest in a cave. It was a deep cave, so deep, in fact, that Saul could not see David and his followers inside, hiding in an alcove.

"This is your chance," David's men told him. "The Lord has brought Saul into your power so that you can kill him."

David nodded and crept close. But he could not bring himself to plunge his knife into the unsuspecting king. Instead he cut off a piece of Saul's robe and silently stole back to his men. Then, when Saul left the cave, David ran after him and threw himself on the ground before him. He held up the piece he had cut from the royal robe.

"People say I plot against you," said David. "But they lie. Here is proof that I could have killed you back there in the cave, but I would not."

*Wide World*

Soldiers explore the cave where David hid from King Saul.

The Bible story reports that Saul then "wept and was ashamed." He told David that any man who was able to return good for evil in that way was sure to be king of Israel. And Saul was right. David became the next king of Israel and one of the great men of history.

Not far from Ein Gedi are the caves where the

Jews of Palestine made their last stand against the Romans. That was about 1,200 years after the glorious reign of David.

The first caves were dug into a blood red mountain called Masada. Here, between 37 and 30 B.C., the Roman ruler Herod built a fantastic three-story fortress over a chain of caves connected by underground passages. There were 40 towers from which watchmen could see the enemy coming from any direction. The caves were jammed with arms, wine, oil, grain, dates, and water. The plan was that anyone in the fortress could retreat to the caves at the first sign of trouble and hide almost indefinitely.

As it happened, Herod never had to use his fortress. But a hundred years later, when Jerusalem itself was captured by the Romans, a thousand Jewish men, women, and children took refuge at Masada. They hid there for three years, with the men sneaking out now and then to harass the Romans. Finally the Romans decided on an all-out attack. They sent an army of 10,000 men to the mountain and set the fortress on fire.

That night as flames burned overhead, Eliezer, leader of the Jews, gathered his people together in the biggest cave. He said the situation was hopeless.

"All we have left," said he, "is one choice. Shall we live as slaves of the Romans or die as free men?"

The Jews voted to kill themselves rather than be slaves. Next day, when the Romans, armed to the hilt, climbed the rampart to the smoldering fortress, they were met by a terrible silence.

The last of the Jewish revolts took place 60 years after the fall of Masada. This was in another group of caves in the deep gorge through which the Jordan falls into the Dead Sea. The leader of this revolt was called Bar Kochba. He and his men were the last survivors of hundreds of thousands of Jews who were killed fighting the Romans.

These caves were not explored until 1961. They are in such a rugged area that the archaeologists had to organize their work like a military operation. With the help of the Israel Defense Forces, the scientists used helicopters to pinpoint the location of the caves. Then men were lowered by ropes from the top of the gorge, while walkie-talkies gave directions from below. Once in the caves, the men used mine detectors to find weapons and copper pans that had been hidden there.

To the great joy of the archaeologists, 60 papyrus scrolls were found in the caves. One contained written orders from Bar Kochba to two of his captains. The archaeologists found remains of some warriors, their skulls piled in baskets. Perhaps most interesting of all, they found Roman coins with the imprinted heads of their gods scratched out. Probably Bar Kochba and his men picked them up in a raid on a Roman camp.

The 15-year-old boy climbed through this entrance to the cave.

# 6. A Boy Makes a Find

The most important of the Jordan River caves so far is the one discovered in 1947 by a 15-year-old Arab boy named Muhammed the Wolf.

Muhammed was tending goats at Qumran, in northwestern Jordan, not far from the caves where Bar Kochba and his men hid. One of the goats wandered off the path and Muhammed threw a stone at it. The stone missed and fell into a hole in a cliff, and Muhammed heard something break.

These openings lead to the cave of the Dead Sea scrolls.

He climbed down to see what it was. He found himself in a cave full of clay jars, one of which had been smashed by his stone. Lying among the pieces was a rolled-up blackish scroll that smelled very bad. Muhammed found six more scrolls in the other jars. He had no idea what they were, but he thought he might sell them to make some money. So he and a friend took them to a merchant in Bethlehem who paid them a modest sum. Then Muhammed went back to his goats.

Muhammed's discovery turned out to be one of the most important finds ever made. It was the first sample of an entire ancient library hidden away by a group of Jews called Essenes, who had been wiped out by the Romans. Practically nothing had been known about them. Now, thanks to the stone thrown by the Arab boy, we know how the Essenes lived, what they believed, and what they thought was going to happen to the world.

The first hint of the importance of the ancient scrolls came from an elderly Jewish archaeologist named E. L. Sukenik. He heard about them soon after they turned up in Bethlehem. Arabs and Jews were fighting for control of Palestine at the time, and Bethlehem was in Arab territory. Going

Pieces of linen wrapping (left) and a clay jar in which the Dead Sea scrolls were found.

*Wide World*

there was dangerous for a Jew, but Sukenik disguised himself as an Arab and went anyhow. He found the merchant who had the scrolls and managed to buy three for $141.

When Sukenik finally got a good look at his purchases, he nearly collapsed. The scrolls were written in ink in Hebrew on thin leather sheets called parchment. They were about eight feet long and in good condition. For nearly 2,000 years the dry air of the cave had preserved them. One of the scrolls was a copy of the Old Testament book of Isaiah. That made it the oldest known Biblical manuscript, a full thousand years older than any other Hebrew text in existence.

Before he could complete his studies of the scrolls, Sukenik died. He had known that four other scrolls had been found and was very disappointed that he had not been able to buy these, too. Then a curious thing happened. Sukenik's son Yigael, who had taken the last name Yadin, was chief of the Israeli army, but he was also an archaeologist. In 1954 Yadin happened to be in

Men inspect the caves where ancient scrolls were found.
Hulton Press Ltd.—Black Star

the United States. One day he picked up a New York newspaper and noticed an advertisement that made his skin prickle. It offered "Four Dead Sea Scrolls" for sale. They were the other scrolls found by the Arab boy. However, in the course of their journey to the United States, the scrolls had gone up in price. The seller now wanted a quarter of a million dollars.

With the help of a generous American, Yadin paid the price and took the scrolls back to Israel. To hold the scrolls the nation of Israel has built one of the most unusual museums ever designed. It is a beautiful, mysterious, cave-shaped building dug into the earth. It is kept at just the right temperature to continue to preserve the manuscripts.

In the meantime, archaeologists from other countries explored other caves near the Dead Sea. They found nearly 600 more fragments and manuscripts in eleven other caves on what is now the Jordan side of the river. They found remains of a village much like the monasteries in which the monks of the Middle Ages worked. There was a

**It takes careful work to piece together the fragments of scrolls.**

place where the scrolls were written. There was a small kiln where the jars that held them were baked. The seals on the jars were made of bitumin from the Dead Sea.

The government of Jordan has set aside the whole area as a national park. In 1965 Jordan loaned some of its scrolls to the Smithsonian Institution for a traveling exhibit that took the scrolls all over the United States. There is a beautiful museum for the scrolls in Jordan, too, which Americans helped build.

In both Israel and Jordan, scholars of every nationality study the precious manuscripts. So far

**Dead Sea scrolls are exhibited in the museum in Jerusalem.**

they have learned that the Essenes were very religious men who left their city homes to live together in the desert near the Dead Sea. They not only preached goodness but practiced it. If one so much as spoke an unkind word to a companion, his food ration was cut for a year. The Essenes spent their time copying the Bible and writing down their beliefs.

How did the Essene library get into the caves in the first place? Scholars think that the Essenes must have learned that the Romans were coming. Instead of hiding themselves, they must have hurried to put away their sacred manuscripts in the safest places they could find. They hid them so well that the scrolls and the Essenes were nearly forgotten for thousands of years.

What the Essenes taught, however, did live on. Not too long afterward, a message of brotherly love and peace much like that of the Essenes was being taught once more in the Jordan Valley. This time the teacher was a poor Jewish carpenter named Jesus, who lived beside the Sea of Galilee.

The dome of Jerusalem's museum which houses the Dead Sea scrolls is modeled after the top of the jar in which the scrolls were found.

*Leni Sonnenfeld*

*Trans World Airlines Photo*

Fishermen at dawn on the Sea of Galilee.

# 7. The Fish of Galilee

The Sea of Galilee has a small flatfish with a big head and a crest. It is called a comb fish and is as interesting a fish as you can find.

The only other place in the world where it exists is the Nile River. The historian Josephus actually believed that there was a tunnel between the Nile and the Sea of Galilee. He thought that the fish swam through it.

But there are even more unusual stories connected with the comb fish, for it is the fish that figures in the life of Jesus.

Jesus grew up beside the Sea of Galilee. One day He heard that His cousin John had become a preacher. John was living in the south, near the Dead Sea, so Jesus decided to go there and hear what he had to say.

He found John on the banks of the Jordan River, surrounded by followers. Like many people in those days, John believed that flowing water washed away sin. So he washed his followers in the Jordan before he preached to them that a Messiah, or Saviour, was soon to come to the earth. This washing is called baptism. Jesus asked to be baptized, too. At first John refused. He looked into the face of Jesus and saw something that made him say that it was Jesus who should be baptizing him. But when Jesus asked him a second time, John dipped Him in the river.

After His baptism, Jesus went into the desert.

He stayed there alone for 40 days, thinking and praying. When He came out of the desert, He had decided upon a new mission. He would preach love, peace, and brotherhood. In some ways, His message was like the teachings of the Essene sect of Jews, who lived nearby. But the teachings of Jesus were to change the world.

Jesus began His preaching at home among the nine thriving towns lining the Sea of Galilee. He found His first followers among the fishermen who made their living catching the comb and other fish that live in the wide blue lake. He saw them casting their nets from the shore and said, "Follow me, and I will make you fishers of men." And they put aside their nets and went with Him.

When Jesus got to Capernaum, one of the busiest of the Galilee towns, He was asked to pay a tribute, or tax. He had no money with Him, so He told His follower Peter to go to the sea, cast a hook, and "take up the fish that first comes up." When Peter opened the mouth of the fish, Jesus said, he would find a coin in it, enough to pay the tax for both of them. Peter caught the

Israeli fishermen prepare their craft for the day's work.

fish and found the coin. The fish that took the
hook was a comb fish. That is why the comb fish
is sometimes called Saint Peter's fish.

As Jesus preached, His fame spread. Sometimes
He spoke from the shore of the Sea of Galilee. At
other times, so many people crowded to hear Him
that He spoke from a fishing boat anchored in
the lake. It was said that He performed many

miracles. He walked on the sea; He quieted waves with a word during a storm; He healed the sick; He even brought the dead back to life.

One of the pleasantest miracles is said to have taken place at the lake town of Tabgha. Some 5,000 men, many with their wives and children, came to hear Him preach. They were so interested that they remained long past their mealtime. Jesus did not want to send them home hungry, but His followers told Him they did not begin to have

Fishermen on the Sea of Galilee bring in their nets.

**Christ feeding the multitude.**

food for such a crowd. They had only five loaves of bread and two small fishes. Jesus told them not to worry but to start passing out the loaves and the fishes. They did, and the more they passed out, the more they had. Finally with all of the crowd fed, they still had food left in their baskets. In a fourth-century church still standing at Tabgha today, a lovely mosaic shows the loaves and the two fishes quite clearly. These are comb fish.

According to the New Testament written by Saint John, the last time Jesus was seen on earth He was cooking fish from the Sea of Galilee. He laid a fire of coals on the shore, and He invited His faithful followers to share the fish with Him.

Hundreds of years later, the followers of Jesus were persecuted by the Romans. To identify themselves to each other they made a secret sign in the dust. It was a drawing of a fish.

The Via Dolorosa in Jerusalem by which Jesus walked to Golgotha.

# 8. The Horns of Hittin

As the teachings of Jesus spread, pilgrims began to come to the Jordan Valley to see the places where He had lived. They called His homeland the Holy Land. It had always been sacred to the Jews. Now it was sacred to the followers of Jesus, who called themselves Christians. Christians came by the thousands, even after the Holy Land was conquered by the Arabs in A.D. 636.

These Arabs had become Muslims, followers of a new religion called Islam. It had been proclaimed by an Arab prophet named Mohammed. Muslims also considered Jerusalem, capital of the Holy

Land, a sacred city. Their religion taught that Mohammed had been taken to heaven from Jerusalem. But the Arabs were perfectly willing to share Jerusalem with the Jews and the Christians.

After several hundred years, however, Kurds, Turks, and other people took over Palestine. They came to be known as Saracens. They adopted Islam as their religion. Then they decided that only Muslims could come to Jerusalem and the Holy Land. Just about the time they came to this decision, a strong-minded French Christian, called Peter the Hermit, arrived in Palestine. When he came within sight of Jerusalem, he learned that all pilgrims were being turned away from the gates of the city. Peter was outraged. He went back to Europe and raised an army to fight against the Saracens so that the Christians might control the Holy Land. Each man wore a cross of red material. These soldiers were Crusaders, a name based on the Latin word for "cross."

The Crusaders and the Saracens fought many bloody battles. First the Saracens won. Then the Crusaders did. The slaughter went on for generations. Finally, between July 2 and July 4 in 1187, a Saracen army led by Saladin defeated the Crusaders at the Horns of Hittin, a ridge overlooking the Sea of Galilee. Historians consider this battle one of the most important ever fought. The days of the battle were broiling hot. The Saracens set fire to the underbrush, and choking smoke floated up. The Crusaders could look down and see the cool blue waters of the Sea of Galilee and the green ribbon of the Jordan flowing out of it. It made them feel thirstier than ever.

Finally, utterly exhausted, the Crusaders surrendered. Saladin was a gallant victor. He decreed that the Christians were free to come and go as they pleased. For all his generosity, however, Saladin had broken the power of the Crusaders. After the victory of the Horns of Hittin, the Christians were never again able to control the Holy Land or any part of the Saracen empire.

They did try again. King Richard of England came to see if he could win the Holy Land back from Saladin. All he actually won was a nickname. He fought Saladin so bravely with inferior forces that he was called "Richard the Lion-Hearted" from that time on.

However, Richard could not seem to defeat Saladin. At one point, Richard offered to send his army back to England if only Saladin would give him Jerusalem and the land west of the Jordan River. Saladin's son, El Adil, in turn, suggested that Richard marry his sister Joanna so that the land could be given to him as a wedding present. Richard agreed, but Joanna flatly refused to marry anyone who was not a Muslim.

The Saracens and Crusaders renewed their fighting, and again Richard was so brave that Saladin and his son could not help admiring him. They stopped the battle and under a flag of truce rode into the Crusader camp to congratulate him. Not to be outdone, Richard invited the pair to dinner. They enjoyed the food very much. They should have, for it had been captured from the Saracen camp just the day before.

Obviously, neither side had much heart left for fighting. The Jordan Valley passed to rulers who often had little interest in its welfare. Greedy

local governors robbed its poor villagers. Land-
lords who never even saw the fields they owned
neglected them. Forests were cut down, goats ate
the hillsides bare, towns were built and abandoned.
Until the end of the last century, there were no
paved roads in the country. Most of the good
roads that remained had been built in Roman days.

But while conquerors came and went, one way
of life continued as it had been when Abraham,
father of the Jews, first crossed the River Jordan
with his family, his flocks, and his tents. That
was the life of the Bedouins, the desert Arabs.

An oasis in dry, desolate Negev country.

*Israel Information Services*

The camel takes a rest while Bedouins make camp in the Negev.

# 9. Tent Dwellers in the Desert

The most colorful people in the Jordan Valley today are the Bedouins, Arabs who roam the wild desert country. Most other Arabs are farmers. Two-thirds of the nearly two million Arabs who live in Jordan work from dawn to dusk on their small plots of land. Most of the quarter of a million Arabs still living on Israel's side of the Jordan River live in square blue-painted houses in farm villages. But close to 200,000 Jordanian

Arabs and 30,000 Israeli Arabs are Bedouins. They prefer the desert way of life to life in any village or city. Their homes are their tents, more dear than any house could be. Many of these tent dwellers spend the winter in the lowlands around the Dead Sea, moving on in the spring. When they are near towns, some even light their tents with electricity. Other Bedouins, especially those in Galilee, live in villages during the winter. They only take to the open desert after the rainy season. Proud and free, the Bedouins go where they please. The sands cover their traces. Occasionally they scratch their *wasm*, or tribal mark, on wells or other landmarks to show that the tribe owns them.

Bedouin life has changed little in 4,000 years. Each tribe has its own leader, or sheik, who makes decisions, protects the weak, receives guests. Princely sheiks may have private armies of handsome Arab horsemen carrying silver daggers, like characters in a motion picture. Others scrape together a hard living for themselves.

Bedouin dress is changeless, too. The men wear

ankle-length black or brown camel's hair cloaks over long-sleeved white shirts. They cover their heads with rectangular cloths called *kafiyyas*, held in place with goat's hair ropes.

Women wear several long, loose robes, tucked in with a wide belt. They paint their eyes with black. Usually Bedouin women go barefoot, but they feel quite undressed without tinkling necklaces, earrings, nose rings, bracelets, armlets, ankle chains, and coins that hang from their foreheads. Jewelry is a Bedouin woman's bank account.

Bedouins earn their living raising sheep, goats,

Bedouin men wear long black or brown robes over white shirts.

A Bedouin mother and
her baby.

*Leni Sonnenfeld*

horses, and camels. As soon as a boy is old enough,
he begins to herd the sheep and goats. Bedouin
girls help their mothers, who do most of the tribe's
work. The men tend the camels.

The camels we see in the zoo look pretty mangy,
but life in the desert would be impossible without
these remarkable beasts. Camels live where all
other livestock would die. They can go without
water for weeks and digest the roughest, thorniest
scrub. Camels provide so much of the Bedouin
transportation that they are called "the ships of
the desert." They furnish food, medicine, and cos-

Young Bedouin shepherds watch their herd of camels.

metics. And if cash is needed, a camel always brings a good price. The owner of a good camel is as proud of him as an American is of his car. Next to protecting his tribe, caring for a camel is considered the only fit occupation for a free son of the desert. The men even milk the camels. They have to. Camels are so bad-tempered that the job is too dangerous for a woman.

From a distance, Bedouin life looks romantic. Close up, it is far less satisfactory. The women

A feast of rice and lamb is served on the rug of the tent.

work too hard and look it. Babies are sickly. Children get little or no schooling since they are always on the move.

The government of Jordan sends mobile health clinics to the Bedouins and tries to get the children to school. It teaches farming. In 1953, King Husayn gave 2,000 acres of rich Jordan Valley land to descendants of tribes who had fought under his great-grandfather, Sherif Husayn. Israel also is trying to help its Bedouins to settle down.

A Bedouin desert
dweller in Jordan.

But making Bedouins settle down is not simple. Hard though life is, it is free. The women enjoy the crafts they pass on to their daughters. The men tell stories around the campfires. Every job has its own song.

No people enjoy having guests more. It is hard to pass a Bedouin tent without having to drink a cup of thick Turkish coffee. At mealtime, a sheep will be killed, even if the tribe itself has been living on roasted locusts and camel's milk. Among wealthy Bedouins, feasts of rice and boiled lamb (called *mansafs*) may go on for days. In the great lonely stretches of the desert, strangers must help each other, so hospitality has become a sacred duty. Even enemies may live in an Arab tent city for three days, once they have broken bread.

It is not easy—nor always wise—to break old patterns. Even the World Health Organization and the International Labor Organization, which are trying to help the Bedouins, say the results are "not very encouraging." As soon as they think a tribe has settled down, it is off again. Like the shepherds of old, the Bedouins seem to think of their God as a shepherd who will always lead them to "green pastures" and "still waters." They never worry about what tomorrow will bring.

**With camel and donkeys loaded, the Bedouin is ready to move on.**
*United Nations*

Young immigrants
arrive at Haifa.
*Leni Sonnenfeld*

# 10. Mother of Kibbutzim

For the Bedouins, roaming is a cherished way
of life. But the Jews who began to come back to
their ancient land early in this century were tired
of wandering. They longed for a permanent home.

In 1909 a dozen young Jews came from Eastern
Europe to settle near the Jordan River just south
of the Sea of Galilee. Like our own American
pioneers who went west to build a new country in
the wilderness, they faced many hardships. The

80

hills overlooking the river, which had been thick with trees in the time of Jesus, were now barren rock. Swamps were infested with mosquitoes. In winter, floods turned dirt roads into mud. In summer, the empty valley reflected the broiling sun like a hot plate. If an experienced farmer had been asked to plant crops and raise cattle there, he would have called the idea crazy. But the young Jewish pioneers knew nothing about farming since Jews in their old country had not been allowed to own land. They had no idea the task was impossible, so they staked out a farm, named it *Degania*, meaning "cornflower," and got to work.

First, they put aside their European clothes and wore red Arab shoes, headcloths, and robes. Then they planted eucalyptus trees to absorb some of the swamp water. They dug irrigation channels. From dawn until sunset, they plowed and carted stones. The Arabs had a story that when God made the world, he forgot stones and sent an angel down with two bagfuls. One of the bags broke over Galilee so half of the world's stones are there. Degania's settlers believed it.

The young Jews set up a system of farming that had never before worked anywhere else. No one got any pay. All money earned went into a common fund to buy food, clothing, and supplies. Everything was shared except their own private lives. Degania was a collective farm or *kibbutz*. Anyone who came to live there had to abide by the same rules.

These rules apply today at Degania and at the 250 other Israeli settlements, or *kibbutzim*, which Degania "mothered." Degania is a good advertisement for the kibbutz method. Its rolling acres are covered with orchards, fertile fields, fishponds, stables, beehives, and the most beautiful gardens in all Israel. Degania built the first bridge across the Jordan River and was the first farm in the Jordan Valley to have three or four crops a year, instead of one or two.

Women at a kibbutz do much the same work as the men, even to working with the animals. Credit for this goes to Miriam Baratz, one of the young founders of Degania. The men had thought the women would stick to housekeeping but Miriam,

*Herbert S. Sonnenfeld*
**Jewish pioneers have made Degania into a beautiful garden.**

whose husband was the first elected leader of Degania, thought share and share alike was only fair. When the settlers got their first cows, Miriam asked to take care of them. The men said it was not proper work for a woman. Miriam sneaked out at night to the nearby Arab village and had the wife of the local sheik teach her to milk. One morning when the men went to the cow barns, they found Miriam beside a row of full pails. Eventually Miriam Baratz became one of the farm experts of her country.

During the difficult early years, the pioneers worried whether babies could survive in the climate. Their babies not only survived but grew up to be tall, tough, sunburned youngsters. Degania's children were the original *sabras*, the name given to the native-born Israeli. Like the *sabra*, or prickly pear, he is said to be "tough on the outside, sweet on the inside."

The children of a kibbutz are very special. They belong to their own parents, of course. But their care is considered the job of the kibbutz. Every kibbutz has at least one children's house, which is usually the best house in the settlement. In the early days, all the children lived, ate, and slept with their own age groups, cared for by trained nurses and teachers while their mothers worked elsewhere on the settlement. Now children sleep in their parents' quarters in many of the kibbutzim. But wherever they live, children and parents visit and play together on certain set hours of the day, after work, and on the Sabbath. Nothing is allowed to interfere with such family time.

Many of Degania's children, however, were not

Children of a kibbutz
are cared for by trained
nurses while their mothers
work. Like the *sabra*
or prickly pear (shown
at right), they are said
to be "tough on the
outside, sweet on the
inside."

*Israel Information Services*

*Leni Sonnenfeld*

In the kibbutz, meals are served in a central dining hall.

born there at all. They were adopted. Since 1934,
Degania and the settlements that followed it have
adopted tens of thousands of homeless, frightened
children. Often this was done with the help of an
American woman, Henrietta Szold, and of Hadassah,
the women's organization she founded.

The homeless children came from Hitler's Germany,
after their parents were put into prison or killed
because they were Jewish. Like the first settlers
of Degania, the children found farm work strange
and had trouble learning Hebrew, the language
spoken on the kibbutz. But inside of two years,

they were so happy and adjusted to the life in Israel that the older ones founded kibbutzim of their own. And when World War II broke out and more children lost home and family, the first German children, now grown, adopted them.

In all, 10,000 children came to the kibbutzim during the war. Many underwent unbelievable hardship. One group of fourteen tattered, starved children turned up at Degania toward the end of the war. They had been on their way for three and a half years. They had escaped from a German prison camp in Poland and made their way through Russia, Siberia, Turkestan, and Persia. They slept in ditches, hid in forests, ate roots and wild berries. All that kept them going was the hope of finding a welcome somewhere. They found it—and more—at Degania. The settlement even provided a mother for them, a gentle, sweet-faced woman whose own daughter had died in a prison camp.

When Israel became an independent state in 1948, by vote of the United Nations, many more homeless children poured into the kibbutzim. They came from Turkey, Bulgaria, Poland, Tunisia, Morocco, Egypt, China, Iraq, Afghanistan, Abyssinia, Libya—nearly a hundred different countries in all. It was the greatest child migration in history. The children were very poor. Some came from villages that had not changed since the fifteenth century. When the Jews of Yemen saw the airplanes that were to take them to Israel, they thought they were giant eagles sent them by God.

**Tractors are used so farming can be done on a large scale.**
*Leni Sonnenfeld*

Harvest time
at Kibbutz Nirim.
*Leni Sonnenfeld*

There were so many new children coming to the kibbutzim that separate children's villages had to be built. Learning new ways was hard for the children. Teaching them was often hard, too. But the sabras of the kibbutzim were patient, for they remembered that their own parents and grandparents had had to learn new ways in a strange land. As they had prospered, the sabras expected these newest children of Israel to prosper too.

P.I.P by Werner Braun

The parched land of the Negev only needs water to be fertile.

# 11. Storm Over the Jordan

It was no accident that the ancient Hebrews had to cross the Jordan to get to their Promised Land of "milk and honey." Without the Jordan, the Promised Land could not have existed. It is still true today. Its waters are vital to the arid countries surrounding it.

All of these countries—Syria, Lebanon, Jordan, and Israel—need water desperately. But instead of cooperating in using their water to the best advantage for all, they fear and distrust each other. Moreover, the Arab countries feel that the land that is now Israel is properly theirs. They will not do anything that helps Israel exist. Both sides of the Jordan have become armed camps.

There is always fighting or the threat of fighting.

Many proposals have been made for division of the Jordan water. Some go back half a century. In 1939 an expert from the United States Department of Agriculture, W. C. Lowdermilk, drew up a master plan for use of the river. It became known as a "T.V.A. on the Jordan." (The initials T.V.A. stand for Tennessee Valley Authority, which has come to mean successful river regulation.)

When Israel became an independent state, it made this proposal the basis of its own national water plan. Eighty-five per cent of Israel's water is in the north, but most of its land is in the south. The Israeli plan takes water from the north to the south. It uses the Sea of Galilee as a reservoir, storing water from winter to summer, from

A Bedouin leads his camels through the arid waste land.
*Wide World*

*Leni Sonnenfeld*            *Leni Sonnenfeld*
108-inch pipe was assembled to bring water from the Jordan.

wet years to dry ones. It takes advantage of the steep drops in the river's course for the generation of electric power. It brings precious water to the desert in the south instead of allowing it to pour, wasted, into the Dead Sea.

The neighboring Arab states are bitterly opposed to Israel's plan. In 1953 President Eisenhower offered to send experts to the area to help draw up a unified water plan that would be acceptable to everyone. The experts worked for two years. Technicians on both sides of the river accepted the unified water plan. But again politics blocked cooperation.

Meanwhile, none of the countries can afford to

Leni Sonnenfeld  Israel Information Services

**Water from the river pours through pipelines and open canals.**

wait for the water they need so badly, so each has gone ahead taking water on its own. Syria and Lebanon are taking water from the Jordan's headwaters. The Kingdom of Jordan is tapping the Yarmuk River, a tributary of the River Jordan. Israel is pumping water from the Sea of Galilee. The Israeli project will bring 84 billion gallons of water a year to the Negev, a dry desolate region in the south.

But the Jordan Valley still needs an accepted plan that will benefit all of its people. President Johnson made a standing offer to help draw up such a plan. "Water should never divide men," he said. "It should unite them. Water should never

Fruits and vegetables flourish when they have enough water.

be a cause of war—it should always be a force for peace."

Meanwhile, the Jordan rolls on. And some day, it may yet be possible to say, as the Bible said in an earlier day, "Lot lifted up his eyes, and he beheld all the Valley of the Jordan. And lo, all of it was irrigated—and it was like a Garden of God."

River water is sprinkled over fields of gladioli in the Negev.

# Index

# Meet the Author

VIOLET WEINGARTEN was born in San Francisco and grew up in New York City. After graduating from Cornell University, she worked as a newspaper reporter. Her assignments included everything from royal visits and murder trials to bagpipe-playing concerts. Now she works with her husband, Victor, in their public relations office. She has written innumerable pamphlets as well as the scripts for several prize-winning motion pictures produced by Mr. Weingarten.

A few years ago, the Weingartens with their two daughters, Jan and Kathy, took a long European trip. They traveled by plane, ship, train, bus, car, gondola, cogtrain, subway, trolley, helicopter and donkey. On their return, Mrs. Weingarten and Kathy, then 13, wrote a book about their travels. In addition, Violet Weingarten has written *The Nile, Lifeline of Egypt*, one of the best sellers in the Rivers of the World Books. It is now being translated into Arabic for publication in the United Arab Republic.

The Weingartens' home is deep in the woods outside Mount Kisco, New York.

## DATE DUE

PLEASE RETURN IN TWO WEEKS

HIGHSMITH    #45102

Leni Sonnenfeld